Grand Canyon
on my mind

66 No matter how far you have wandered hitherto, or how many famous gorges and valleys you have seen, this one, the Grand Canyon of the Colorado, will seem as novel to you, as unearthly in the color and grandeur and quantity of its architecture, as if you had found it…on some other star. 99

John Muir

FALCON®

Like many geologic features in the Canyon, Vishnu Temple reminded early explorers of the ruins of a majestic shrine.
JEFF GNASS

" Nothing prepares you for the Grand Canyon. No matter how many times you read about it or see it pictured, it still takes your breath away. Your mind, unable to deal with anything on this scale, just shuts down and for many long moments you are a human vacuum, without speech or breath, but just a deep, inexpressible awe that anything on this earth could be so vast, so beautiful, so silent. "

Bill Bryson

With an average elevation of more than 8,000 feet, the North Rim is cool and wet enough
to support a mixed forest, including these aspens. JEFF GNASS

Tinajas in the Toroweap area collect rainwater, providing essential moisture for desert wildlife.   GEORGE H. H. HUEY

Dawn's early light burnishes Mount Hayden, a distinctive monolith seen here from the North Rim.   JAMES RANDKLEV

6

The mineral travertine colors the pool below Havasu Falls a brilliant turquoise blue.
JAMES RANDKLEV

66 *It is no wonder that when men first looked upon the river and its canyons, they found in them myths and dreams. The river was a mystery, its canyons too awesome for comprehension, too beautiful for belief.* 99

T. H. Watkins

Clarence E. Dutton, a colleague of John Wesley Powell, named a number of Grand Canyon landmarks, including this overlook known as Cape Final. RANDY PRENTICE

Dense stands of North Rim aspen reawaken in the spring. STEVE MULLIGAN

" *I stood there upon the rim of that tremendous chasm and forgot who I was, and what I came there for. Before me lay the sublimest panorama in the world. Nature never made anything like it anywhere else. It is the great masterpiece.* "

Winfield Hogaboom

Diana Temple towers over Crystal Rapid, a river runner's nightmare in Granite Gorge.   LARRY ULRICH

Dories crowd a prime camping beach in Granite Gorge. LARRY ULRICH

Marble Canyon, on the eastern end of Grand Canyon National Park, was named for its polished limestone walls. LARRY ULRICH

As the day fades, the view from Lipan Point is engulfed in violet shadow. ERIC WUNROW

"As the day draws to a close, shadows, wondrous, black, and thick, like those of the morning, fill up the wall hollows, while the glowing rocks, their rough angles burned off, seem soft and hot to the heart as they stand submerged in purple haze, which now fills the cañon like a sea."

John Muir

The sinuous walls of Matkatamiba Canyon echo the creek that helped to carve them.   RANDY PRENTICE

At Grand Canyon Lodge on the North Rim, you can stand on the
very brink of the abyss. THOMAS E. GAMACHE

The falls of Clear Creek are especially dramatic when snowmelt surges
off the North Rim. BILL HATCHER

Erosion has exposed the full breadth of colossal Redwall Cavern to river runners.   LARRY ULRICH

A kayaker negotiates Forster Rapid in Granite Gorge.
STEPHEN TRIMBLE

    Each wave is a watery lion's paw, playfully smacking a gray mouse of a raft with strength to spare. It is pure river on the river's terms.

Ann Zwinger

Havasu Falls seems magically out of place in this parched desert environment.
JEFF GNASS

Stout-hearted hikers view Mooney Falls from the dizzying trail that leads to the floor of Havasu Canyon.
JAMES RANDKLEV

A fiery sunrise chases shadows from the Canyon's depths.   JAMES RANDKLEV

Rafters in Granite Rapids endure an icy slap in the face.   LARRY ULRICH

A couple enjoys the cool water of Royal Arch Creek at picturesque Elves Chasm Falls.   TOM TILL

Havasu Creek slices northward through the Havasupai Indian Reservation to its union with the Colorado River.
LARRY ULRICH

A canyoneer rappels Deer Creek Falls at the mouth of Deer Creek Canyon in Granite Narrows.
BILL HATCHER

The setting sun warms Vishnu Temple, viewed here from Cape Royal on the North Rim. RANDY PRENTICE

❝ *There are people of a certain spirit who, having looked at the Grand Canyon from the rim, must descend into it. And once they have done so they never forget the experience.* ❞

Robert Wallace

Brahma and Deva Temples provide a muted backdrop for a fiery autumn show of maples. RANDY PRENTICE

An enterprising duo hikes the Bright Angel Trail, a popular thoroughfare
from rim to river. DENNIS FLAHERTY

One of the most widely spread tree species on the continent, the quaking aspen can get by on only 7 inches of water a year.
LARRY ULRICH

Purple penstemons adorn a meadow on the Kaibab Plateau, a high-country oasis surrounded by desert.
JAMES RANDKLEV

❝ From rim to river, in any season, canyon country is worth leaving home for. ❞

Seymour L. Fishbein

The Colorado River flows 62 miles through Marble Canyon, from Lees Ferry to the mouth of the Little Colorado.
LARRY ULRICH

      *As the shadows deepen in the
lower deeps, beginning to wash like
the flood of a spectral purple sea the
gray-green mesas of the lower levels,
then the river's voice swells till it
seems to fill the whole enormous
canyon—savage, solemn and
persistent.*

Hamlin Garland

Coyote and cactus: icons of the Southwest.
CAROL POLICH

Moonlight barely penetrates the upper reaches of the mile-deep Canyon. BILL HATCHER

These petroglyphs lie just outside the northern boundary of Grand Canyon National Park, in Billy Goat Canyon.
ERIC WUNROW

A Hualapai woman passes on the traditions of her people.
STEPHEN TRIMBLE

" Ancient rocks, like old folks, acquire character through endurance of time and adversity, acquire beauty through character. "

Edward Abbey

At Cape Final, a skeletal tree limb and a blooming agave make for a striking canyon still life.   RANDY PRENTICE

The roadrunner feeds on small reptiles, scorpions, insects, and rodents.   JOHN R. FORD

When startled, the desert collared lizard will rise up on its hind legs and run away.   CAROL POLICH

Frost traces the outline of a branch of Gambel oak, whose acorns serve as an important food source for canyon wildlife. RANDY PRENTICE

A classic North Rim scene: an open meadow rimmed by flaming fall foliage.
THOMAS E. GAMACHE

The Kaibab Plateau is world-renowned for its massive mule deer. JOHN R. FORD

" *Look twice, think twice, when you meet autumn on a mountainside. There is sorcery in the season.* **"**

Raymond Carlson

Snow clings like icing to the canyon rim at Yavapai Point and to the summits of Cheops Pyramid and Isis Temple beyond. RANDY PRENTICE

> *Not a solitary sound emerges from those depths. It is as though all the silences and hushes of time beyond imagining have drifted into the Canyon and filled it to the brim.*

Robert Wallace

A juniper takes a curtain call.
RICHARD HAMILTON SMITH

39

A young tree clings to life below the canyon rim.
KATHLEEN NORRIS COOK

66 When you come to the Grand Canyon it's as though Nature were breaking out in supplication.... [I]t is one of the few spots on this earth which not only comes up to expectation but surpasses it. 99

Henry Miller

The Colorado River is the pot of gold at the end of this double rainbow. TOM TILL

Summer storm clouds skate across the sky over Lipan Point. The South Rim gets a scant 15 inches of rain per year. TOM TILL

" *Clouds are playing in the cañon to-day. Sometimes they roll down in great masses, filling the gorge with gloom; sometimes they hang above, from wall to wall, and cover the cañon with a roof of impending storm.... The clouds are children of the heavens, and when they play among the rocks, they lift them to the region above.* "

John Wesley Powell

Ponderosa pines on the South Rim grow up to 100 feet tall, but lack of precipitation stunts the growth of less hardy trees.   CLINT FARLINGER

We wandered along the quietest sylvan path, which led us up and down little ravines and dales, always under the shade of tall pines, always over the brown carpet of their needles. Now and then a sudden chasm would lift a corner of the veil, and we would wonder how we dared go on.

Harriet Monroe

An aspen grows beside a remnant of the volcanic activity that helped shape the Canyon.

THOMAS E. GAMACHE

45

The view to the south from Cape Royal reveals the South Rim, and 70 miles
beyond it, the San Francisco Peaks. THOMAS E. GAMACHE

Built in the early 1930s, the Watchtower offers
spectacular views.
CHRISTIAN HEEB / GNASS PHOTO IMAGES

*" The Canyon... is the most revealing
single page of earth's history anywhere
open on the face of the globe. "*

Joseph Wood Krutch

Daisies blanket a Kaibab Plateau meadow.
TOM TILL

❝ A phenomenon like the Grand Canyon may make a man feel small or it may make him feel large—it does not matter which. The point is that it compels him to feel something, *to respond to his own existence with a force of recognition that the society in which he normally functions cannot inspire. ❞*

T. H. Watkins

49

Thick forests of pinyon pine grow on the Canyon's South Rim. The wetter North Rim (in the distance) hosts mixed conifer and deciduous forests. GEORGE H. H. HUEY

Sunrise and fresh snow accentuate the highly acclaimed beauty of the Grand Canyon.   LAURENCE PARENT

A fringe of ice frames a view from Yavapai Point. RANDY PRENTICE

Even snow cannot blunt a broadleaf yucca. STEVE MULLIGAN

A ponderosa pine cone nestles amid the phlox.
GEORGE H. H. HUEY

A hedgehog cactus erupts with blossoms.
LARRY ULRICH

A yucca blossom emerges from a nest of bayonet-like
leaves.   GEORGE H. H. HUEY

The blossom of a Simpson's hedgehog cactus peeks
from a bed of pine needles.   SCOTT T. SMITH

52

Prickly pear, globemallow, and prince's plume share a niche in Havasu Canyon.   LARRY ULRICH

Dating back 1.8 billion years, Vishnu schist is among the oldest exposed rock in the Canyon.
TOM TILL

Clouds enhance the drama of a brilliant canyon sunset. ERIC WUNROW

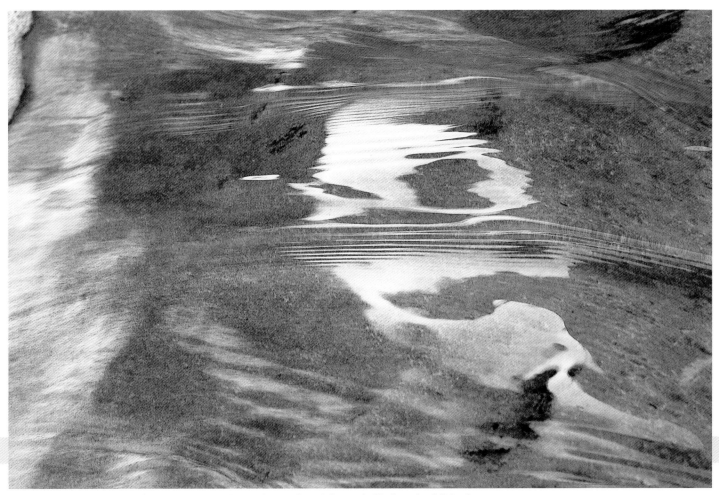

Spring water reflects the walls of Scotty's Hollow in Slide Canyon. BILL HATCHER

Long of claw and stout of body, badgers are built for digging.   TOM & PAT LEESON

In the war of sun and dryness against living things, life has its secrets of survival.

John Steinbeck

The long ears of the black-tailed jackrabbit help to keep it cool.   TOM & PAT LEESON

An American kestrel perches on the stalk of a wooly mullein. TOM & PAT LEESON

The colorful rock layers of the Grand Canyon reveal two billion years of geologic history.   MARK & JENNIFER MILLER

Sheets of rain assault Freya Castle and Vishnu Temple, viewed at dusk from Walhalla Lookout.   RANDY PRENTICE

*" We could hear a thunder shower
reverberating back in some of the valleys of
the Cañon; and the rain falling between us
and the red rocks was as a curtain to the
scene shifting of those old earth and
mountain and water gods hiding in the
wings of the vast amphitheater. "*

Agnes C. Laut

Trail riders have the right-of-way as they pick their way down the Bright Angel Trail. CAROL POLICH

Cautious hikers navigate the nerve-racking trail to Mooney Falls on Havasu Creek. CHEYENNE ROUSE

A pack train heads down Cedar Ridge via the South Kaibab Trail, which leads to the Kaibab Suspension Bridge over the Colorado River. JEFF GNASS

The overlook at Grand Canyon Lodge offers stunning views from the North Rim.
THOMAS E. GAMACHE

You cannot truly comprehend the magnitude of the Grand Canyon until you venture into it. LAURENCE PARENT

A hiker contemplates the Canyon from the rim
at Toroweap. CHEYENNE ROUSE

" To stand upon the edge of this stupendous gorge is to enjoy in a moment compensation for years of uneventful life. "

John L. Stoddard

The Colorado River derives its name from the Spanish word for red. Since the completion of the Glen Canyon Dam in 1963 the river runs clearer, but it still fills with red silt after rainstorms.   TOM TILL

Yaki Point provides a ringside seat for another breathtaking canyon sunset. GEORGE H. H. HUEY

❝ *To see the Grand Canyon full of purple smoke at dawn or sublimely fired at sunset, is to be elevated in soul.* **❞**

Zane Grey

Get ready to get wet! The Colorado claims another raft.   RICHARD HAMILTON SMITH

A river guide maneuvers her craft through Marble Canyon.   LIN ALDER

A fine beach and an opportunity to explore make Redwall Cavern a popular stop for rafters.   KATHLEEN NORRIS COOK

A game of Hacky Sack in Redwall Cavern? Why not?   STEPHEN TRIMBLE

A daring climber takes in South Rim vistas from an unusual perspective. BILL HATCHER

*66 Who could ask for a finer place than our Canyon in which
to taste life deeply by risking life? By hanging it over the edge? 99*

Edward Abbey

Tired of rowing? Try climbing Grapevine Buttress.
BILL HATCHER

Day is done for this hiker at Cape Royal.
MARK & JENNIFER MILLER

Travertine, a mineral leached from limestone, accumulates in Havasu Creek and forms a series of surrealistic falls. JEFF GNASS

Havasu Creek streaks over Mooney Falls, creating an Edenlike oasis in an otherwise harsh landscape.
JEFF GNASS

Havasu Creek cascades over travertine shelves at Beaver Falls.   LIN ALDER

The Little Colorado River flows over travertine formations near its confluence with the Colorado. RANDY PRENTICE

" ... *the incessant, thundering, express-engine roar of the water. In many parts of the canyon it never ceases, day or night. It speeds the heartbeat and deafens the ears and shakes the ground underfoot. It comes from every side, echoed and multiplied by the walls. A man's voice is lost, shouting in it.* *"*

Wallace Stegner

Stantons Cave offers a respite from the searing summer heat of the Inner Gorge.   TOM TILL

Elves Chasm Falls is a short hike up Royal Arch Creek from the Colorado River.   TOM TILL

> *Suddenly, you turn a rock angle, and the yellow, muddy, turbulent flood of the Colorado swirls past you, tempestuous, noisy, sullen and dark, filling the narrow cañon with the war of rock against water.*

Agnes C. Laut

A prickly pear cactus thrives at river's edge, where the temperature can easily be 20 degrees hotter than at the Canyon rim. RANDY PRENTICE

At 6,394 feet, Chuar Butte looms over the confluence of the Colorado and Little Colorado Rivers. LARRY ULRICH

The cool water of Royal Arch Creek in Elves Chasm is a welcome treat for bone-weary river runners.
LIN ALDER

The adventurous put their fate in the hands of a good oarsman.   KATHLEEN NORRIS COOK

Three thousand feet below Toroweap Point, the Colorado River meanders across the Canyon floor.
WILLARD CLAY

The river has the last laugh at Toroweap Point. Just downstream are the fiercest rapids of them all: Lava Falls.
WILLARD CLAY

From the murky depths of the Little Colorado Gorge, the Little Colorado joins forces with its larger relation.
JEFF GNASS

From rim to rim, the Canyon averages 10 miles wide.   STEVE MULLIGAN

The awesome size of the Canyon is readily apparent from the air.
STEVE MULLIGAN

Viewed from Point Imperial on the North Rim, Mount Hayden stands guard as day breaks. JEFF GNASS

All the rocks, as if wild with life, throb and quiver and glow in the glorious sunburst, rejoicing. Every rock temple then becomes a temple of music; every spire and pinnacle an angel of light and song, shouting color halleluiahs.

John Muir

Primed by underground aquifers, Thunder Spring gushes from the canyon wall.   LARRY ULRICH

Navajo Falls is the second of five waterfalls on Havasu Creek below the village of Supai. JEFF GNASS

Mather Point is a popular and often crowded overlook on the South Rim, but the stunning views make it worth braving the multitudes.   JAMES RANDKLEV

The view is just as dramatic at Lipan Point, and the crowds are thinner.   MARK & JENNIFER MILLER

Traditional Navajo rug weavers use the fruit of the
prickly pear to make dye. LARRY ULRICH

A stand of aspens appears to play nursemaid to a young blue spruce.   JEFF GNASS

Beauty comes in all forms, even dried mud.   TOM TILL

Ponderosa pine needles and cones carpet the forest floor on the Walhalla Plateau. The ponderosa is the most abundant pine in the Southwest. JEFF GNASS

The Kaibab squirrel is found only on the Kaibab Plateau.   TOM & PAT LEESON

95

The porcupine is one of 76 species of mammal known to live in or near the Canyon.
TOM & PAT LEESON

Close up, an agave looks forbidding yet
beautiful. SCOTT T. SMITH

66 *I saw the agave now as a part of the
green bedrock of life on earth. As a part of
the plant life that captures for this planet
the energy of the sun....* 99

Colin Fletcher

Indian paintbrush decorates a meadow on the Walhalla Plateau near Cape Final.   RANDY PRENTICE

Autumn-clad aspens surround a solitary ponderosa pine. RANDY PRENTICE

A lava boulder makes a perfect backdrop for these eye-catching desert marigolds.   LARRY ULRICH

Butterfly weed blossoms are true to their name.   CLARK SCHAACK

Wind and rain chiseled Angels Window from the massive outcropping known as Cape Royal. JEFF GNASS

Rebuilt in 1937 following a fire, Grand Canyon Lodge clings to the North Rim at Bright Angel Point. JEFF GNASS

The rising sun throws a spotlight on a sandstone buttress at Cape Royal on the North Rim. JEFF GNASS

The canyon walls rose straight up on either side of us, ranging from sunset orange to deep rust, mottled with purple. The sandstone had been carved by ice ages and polished by desert eons of sandpaper winds. The place did not so much inspire religion as it seemed to be religion itself.

Barbara Kingsolver

> *It is as though to the glory of nature were added the glory of art; as though, to achieve her utmost, the proud young world had commanded architecture to build for her and color to grace the building.*

Harriet Monroe

A hanging garden of monkeyflowers embellishes the canyon wall above Kanab Creek.   LARRY ULRICH

Early canyonland cultures left intriguing signs of their presence, like this ancient pictograph in the Kaibab National Forest. TOM TILL

A wickiup catches the first light of dawn at Eagle Point on the Hualapai Indian Reservation. RANDY PRENTICE

Hopi petroglyphs decorate an outcrop near Moenave, Arizona. STEPHEN TRIMBLE

" Even here, in this inhospitable rock desert, in this place where the earth is gashed open to the dark mile-deep bone, people have made marks, even homes. "

Wallace Stegner

These 1,000-year-old granaries hug the wall of Marble Canyon near the mouth of Nankoweap Creek.
TOM TILL

❝ Facing the morning sun, was a village built into the cliff....
It reminded me of cliff-swallow nests, or mud-dauber nests, or
crystal gardens sprung from their own matrix: the perfect
constructions of nature. ❞

Barbara Kingsolver

Finely crafted works in silver, like this woman's belt, are a Navajo tradition.   STEPHEN TRIMBLE

A Hualapai tour guide holds agave leaves, which his people once used to make hairbrushes.

RANDY PRENTICE

they made it possible

Grand Canyon on My Mind would have been impossible to produce without the keen eyes and technical skills of more than two dozen professional photographers. These women and men submitted their finest images, and the results show in this stunning collection of photos. What does not show is the work it took to get these images—the early mornings to capture the sunrise, the endless hours of waiting for the perfect light, the hundreds of shots that didn't turn out quite right, and the high level of technical skill that was acquired through years of experience and study. To all the photographers who contributed to *Grand Canyon on My Mind,* we say thanks. We appreciate their art and their hard work.

The Publisher

Photographers in *Grand Canyon on My Mind*

Lin Alder
Willard Clay
Kathleen Norris Cook
Clint Farlinger
Dennis Flaherty
John R. Ford
Thomas E. Gamache
Jeff Gnass
Bill Hatcher
George H. H. Huey
Tom and Pat Leeson
Mark and Jennifer Miller
Steve Mulligan
Laurence Parent
Carol Polich
Randy Prentice
James Randklev
Cheyenne Rouse
Clark Schaack
Richard Hamilton Smith
Scott T. Smith
Tom Till
Stephen Trimble
Larry Ulrich
Eric Wunrow
Gnass Photo Images
Christian Heeb

© 2000 by Falcon® Publishing, Inc.
Helena, Montana

All rights reserved, including the right to reproduce any part of this book in any form, except brief quotations for reviews, without the written permission of the publisher.

Design, typesetting, and other prepress work by Falcon Publishing, Helena, Montana
Printed in Korea

1 2 3 4 5 6 7 8 9 0 PP 03 02 01

Library of Congress
Number: 00-130160

ISBN 1-56044-787-7

For extra copies of this book please check with your local bookstore, or write Falcon Publishing, P.O. Box 1718, Helena, MT 59624 or call toll-free 1-800-582-2665.
Visit our web site at: www.falcon.com

FALCON®

AMERICA
on my mind
series

Front cover photos:
Rainbow over O'Neill Butte, RANDY PRENTICE
Prickly pear cactus, LARRY ULRICH

Back cover photos:
View from Mather Point, South Rim, RANDY PRENTICE
Havasu Falls, JAMES RANDKLEV
Havasupai children on horse, ERIC WUNROW
Boats in Matkatamiba Canyon, LARRY ULRICH

End papers: Sunrise on Osiris Temple, WILLARD CLAY
Page Layout: MICHAEL CUTTER
Project Editor: GAYLE SHIRLEY
Text research: ROB BREEDING

acknowledgments

The Publisher gratefully acknowledges the following sources:

Title page quote from "The Wild Parks and Forest Reservations of the West," by John Muir. *Atlantic Monthly,* January 1898.

Page 3 quote from *The Lost Continent: Travels in Small-Town America,* by Bill Bryson. New York: Harper & Row, 1989.

Pages 7, 48, 75, and 107 quotes from *The Grand Colorado: The Story of a River and Its Canyons,* by T. H. Watkins and Contributors. Palo Alto: American West Publishing Company, 1969.

Page 9 quote from "To the Grand Canyon on an Automobile," by Winfield Hogaboom. *Los Angeles Herald Illustrated Magazine,* February 2, 1902.

Pages 13 and 87 quotes from "The Grand Canyon of the Colorado," by John Muir. *Century Illustrated Monthly Magazine,* November 1902.

Page 17 quote from *Run, River, Run,* by Ann Zwinger. New York: Harper & Row, 1975.

Pages 24 and 39 quotes from *The Grand Canyon,* by Robert Wallace and the Editors of Time-Life Books. New York: Time-Life Books, 1972.

Page 27 quote from *Grand Canyon Country: Its Majesty and Its Lore,* by Seymour L. Fishbein. Washington, DC: National Geographic Society, 1991.

Page 29 quote from "The Grand Canyon at Night," by Hamlin Garland, in *The Grand Canyon of Colorado,* by C.A. Higgins et al. Santa Fe: The Passenger Department of the Santa Fe Railroad, 1906.

Page 33 quote from *The Hidden Canyon: A River Journey,* by Edward Abbey. New York: Penguin Books, 1977.

Page 37 quote from *Arizona's Scenic Seasons,* by Raymond Carlson. Phoenix: Arizona Department of Transportation, 1984.

Page 40 quote from *The Air-Conditioned Nightmare,* by Henry Miller. New York: New Directions, 1945.

Page 43 quote from *First Through the Grand Canyon,* by John Wesley Powell. New York: Outing Publishing Company, 1915.

Pages 45 and 104 quotes from "The Grand Canyon of the Colorado," by Harriet Monroe. *Atlantic Monthly,* December 1899.

Page 47 quote from *Grand Canyon, Today and All Its Yesterdays,* by Joseph Wood Krutch. New York: William Sloane Associates, 1958.

Page 56 quote from *Travels with Charley,* by John Steinbeck. New York: Viking, 1962.

Pages 61 and 78 quotes from *Through Our Unknown Southwest,* by Agnes C. Laut. New York: McBride, Nast & Company, 1913.

Page 65 quote from *John L. Stoddard's Lectures: Southern California, Grand Canyon, Yellowstone Park,* by John L. Stoddard. Boston: Balch Brothers, 1900.

Page 67 quote from "An Appreciation of the Grand Canyon," by Zane Grey, in *Picturesque America, Its Parks and Playgrounds,* ed. by John Kane. New York: Resorts and Playgrounds of America, 1925.

Page 70 quote from *Down the River,* by Edward Abbey. New York: E. P. Dutton, 1982.

Page 96 quote from *The Man Who Walked Through Time,* by Colin Fletcher. New York: Alfred A. Knopf, 1968.

Pages 103 and 108 quotes from *Animal Dreams,* by Barbara Kingsolver. New York: HarperPerennials, 1991.

Page 112 quote from "The Grand Canyon of the Colorado," by John Burroughs. *Century Illustrated Monthly Magazine,* January 1911.

Nowhere does the sun rise and set more gloriously than in the Grand Canyon.
KATHLEEN NORRIS COOK

*❝ I am sure that the remainder of our lives will be the
richer for our having seen the Grand Cañon. ❞*

John Burroughs